Dr. Laura
Gets on My Nerves

Dr. Laura
Gets on My Nerves

An Approach to Morality without Smugness

By
Traci M. Christian

Leathers Publishing
4500 College Blvd.
Leawood, KS 66211
1 / 800 / 888-7696

CONTENTS

INTRODUCTION

I WAS DRIVING in my car today, listening to Dr. Laura on the radio. I catch her show whenever I can. She was touting a new book, and curiously it wasn't one of her own. It is called "Why I Love Dr. Laura." It's available through a website, and now through Dr. Laura's website. Well, of course she was just thrilled that the author of the book — I don't remember his name — had taken criticisms of her and responded to them in a most wonderful way. She cutely commented on how thin the book was in light of the many volumes of criticisms out there and joked in her usual fashion. I can't imitate the high-pitched cackle in a book, but loyal listeners will know the tone: "Oh! Fewer people are aborted because of her! What a bitch! …. What do I do that's so evil?"

I decided to write this for several reasons, not the least of which is to put down that straw-man defense that I've heard so often from Dr. Laura. You know what I mean by straw man, right? That's when you take the opposing point and blow it way out of proportion, then attack the twisted version as though it were the real thing. For example, when a recent caller was talking about how she believed that the few hours a week that she spends away from home makes her a better mother, Dr. Laura cut her off with that cackle: "Oh yes! I'm a better mother because I spend 12 hours a day away from my children!" Twelve hours a week is quite different from twelve hours a day, but then that would not have helped make Dr. Laura's point. Personally I cringe every time I hear her use this defense. I think she is simply too intelligent to need it! With a little effort, she could respond to actual constructive criticism without distorting it way out of proportion. Now, I'm no psychologist-type, but it seems to me that this overdefensiveness is a sign of fear. Smugness also is a sign of fear. I just don't know whether it's a fear that her own moral structure might be harmed by critics (this seems a little silly, knowing how persuaded by her own convictions she is) or if it's a fear that her listeners might be swayed by criticisms of her. I'm guessing it's both, but more the former. I would think that someone who has been so open to so many millions of people, and who has the loyal following that she does, would have learned by now that it's not necessary to brand all of her critics as "stupid." It's not necessary to take an opposing point, distort it and then run it into the ground just to make her own point valid.

I do not believe that Dr. Laura is evil. If you are reading this hoping that I will just bash her mercilessly, you will be disappointed. I think that she is basically a good person trying to do good things. There are ways in which I think she could be a better moral leader, and I will elaborate on that. And there are specific issues on which she and I disagree. On specific issues, I want to give my opinion and explain how my view on an issue fits with my spiritual and moral belief system. I still respect her opinion, but I want to explain another approach to looking at things. It does not

FEMINISM

"FEMINISM" has become such a dirty word in conservative circles. What exactly does it mean anymore? I think that if you ask Dr. Laura, you will most likely get what I call the "Rush Limbaugh definition." It's an image of women in combat boots with short hair and no makeup ready to rip the arm off of the first poor slob who tries to open the door for them, an image of women who think that all men are pigs, all sex is rape and that women can do absolutely *anything* better than men can. Where are these women, anyway? Somebody's been watching too much television. This is, of course, your standard straw-man tactic. Create an image loosely based on the real thing, but with a lot of extraneous negative traits mixed in. Then proceed to attack it as though it really *were* the real thing. Makes for some dramatic dialogue, but really gets us nowhere because no one is talking about the real thing anymore. So what is the real thing? What does your average feminist look like? Would you know one if you saw one?

I claim that her image has evolved over the years since she first emerged. It's an image that has changed with each decade. And like any evolving species, time is needed to weed out the undesirable characteristics and to have remaining the traits and skills needed to survive and thrive.

I don't call the earliest turn-of-the-century crusaders for women's rights — the right to vote, own property, etc. "feminists" per se. They belong in a completely separate league. I think that the first feminists emerged after World War II. The war was over, and Rosie the Riveter was sent home. My grandmother worked in a sheet metal division of an airplane factory during the war. Her generation of women in the '40s were out to prove to themselves and to the country that, as the poster declared, "We Can Do It." And so they did. But then, of course, the war ended, and the men came home. That was a good thing, yes, but it was the beginning of a feeling of resentment among women who were now being asked to forget their accomplishments on the outside and return home to cooking, cleaning and raising children. Most of them went, if not all enthusiastically, because it was expected and also because the jobs that they had held were now closed to them. Many, if not most, job ads after the war read "women need not apply."

A friend once told me that his mother got a part-time job in the '40s to help pay bills. His father worked as an insurance salesman. One day his father went to work and was confronted by his boss. He was informed that if his wife did not quit her job and return home, he would be fired. The logic was that a man who had some other source of income would not work as hard at selling insurance.

It's not that the women minded the cooking and cleaning and child-rearing — they had become accustomed to doing all three while still working outside the home. It was just that they felt like they had spread their wings and were flying to new heights, only to have them clipped by the returning men.

The '50s were a brewing and stewing time. Women

only the progress of women in this country, but also the progress of blacks and other minorities. I have heard Oprah Winfrey make similar comments on her television show and I agree. The envy of our peers can sometimes make us our worst enemy. It can be most destructive.

Modern conveniences left women with more *time* in their days — time to realize that there was more to life than just homemaking. This is not at all to say that homemaking is or ever was a bad thing. Most women would have told you then as they would now that raising their children was their most rewarding and proudest achievement. I suppose that this is the main point on which I disagree with Dr. Laura: the idea that a woman can thoroughly enjoy raising her children — and still need more, want more and be capable of more. And still raise her children! I'll cover this subject in more detail in another chapter.

Anyway, back to the chronology of feminism. The '60s did see some extreme moments in the evolution of feminism. There will always be those who get a little carried away. But then, without those who get carried away and really push things, we don't see the great strides.

The feminists of the '70s were the ones who really pushed their way into corporate and industrial America. It was the time of the "Enjoli" perfume woman. You remember her? "I can bring home the bacon ... Fry it up in a pan! ... And never, never, never let you forget you're a man! ... 'Cuz I'm a *Woooooooman!*" This was one of those times when things had gone a bit too far in my opinion. It was the age of the Superwoman complex. Homemaking was portrayed as a secondary and sometimes even second-class occupation. Many women wanted to be defined by a career role first and as wives and mothers second. The most important reason for this was because women were finally coming to a place in society where they could financially support themselves and their children if the need arose.

I'm always amused at people who want to return to the "good ole days" — the days when women knew their place and didn't invade those places and situations where men exerted their authority. Let's face it, until about 30 or so years ago, men in this country and pretty much the world were running the show. Even if a marriage had problems such as adultery, addiction or abuse (Dr. Laura's three A's — acceptable reasons for ending a marriage), most women could not afford to divorce. I claim that divorces increased in this country not because feminists decided that they no longer wanted to remain married — I expect that women had been wanting out of bad marriages for centuries! It was just that now they had more options and could actually do something about it.

The problem was that women expected themselves and each other to be able to do both a career and homemaking without a hitch. While I don't think that this was a healthy place for feminism to be either, I understand it as a step along the way. It's been said that a woman has to work twice as hard as a man in order to get half the recognition. I think that this was true, at least back then. In order for women to prove themselves in the workplace, they had to accomplish great things on the job and still maintain their home life. It became acceptable, and common, to place young children in full-time day care and to pursue career goals.

In the '80s, placing children in day care was almost expected. By the time the '80s rolled around, women had successfully opened most of the workplace doors, even though they were still earning a fraction of the salaries at the same jobs as men had, but things were looking up.

Unfortunately, it was still taking some pretty extreme measures to bring down all of the old stereotypes. Again, not the ideal place for us to be, but still a step in the right direction. The '80s era of greed fueled the image of homemaking as a secondary career. Women were still expecting of themselves and each other that they would advance to the top of their careers and still hold the home life together — again, without a hitch.

It doesn't surprise me that during the '60s , '70s and '80s some resentment toward men developed in the feminist movement. I can understand a woman being a little perturbed at working her butt off while the man in the cubicle next to her produced half as much and received twice the pay. If you don't believe that happened and *still* happens, you are fooling yourself. And some of the resentment did get out of hand. After all, a single generation of men could not be blamed for the way that the world had been clicking along after several thousand years, especially when most men didn't see what was so bad about it!

But times have changed. The granddaughters of the Rosies and the daughters of the bra burners are now the up-and-coming feminists of today. We have learned a lot from hearing and reading about the past. And we're teaching our mothers and even our grandmothers a thing or two about feminism. The movement is still evolving. Feminism today looks nothing like it did 30, 20 or even 10 years ago. To bash feminists, as Dr. Laura does, on the basis of a definition out of the '60s , '70s or '80s , is to be out of touch and uninformed.

There are feminists today staying home to raise their children. Feminists get married every day — because, you see, we *like* men! But, the men we are marrying today were raised by women who persisted through much more discrimination and repression than we will ever face. The men we are marrying were raised by women who wanted them to view their mothers, their sisters and their wives in a different light. And so they do. They are doing more housework and taking a greater role in raising the children. They are also sometimes finding it necessary to explain to their fathers why they will be present at the births of their children. Also, since they are married to us modern feminists, they understand the importance of equity in the workplace.

Today's feminists are enjoying the fruits of the labors of their mothers and grandmothers. We still encounter discrimination, but there are new avenues, already paved, that we can take to rectify it. Since we have not faced the same kind of blatant discrimination that was commonplace in past generations, we do not harbor the same resentments toward men. We are holding ourselves responsible and accountable for where we are today and where we are going. The life choices we make are really up to us now. Almost all of the limitations from past generations are now gone. There are still a few extremists in the feminist movement today, but the majority of today's feminists stand for personal responsibility, not victimhood. Women were once victims of a discriminatory society, but that is not the case anymore in most places in this country, and we realize that.

I once heard a male caller on Dr. Laura's show talking about how his wife had suddenly and unexpectedly left him and his children. Dr. Laura was probing him for reasons why and asked if the woman had been reading any feminist literature recently. Her reasoning was that the woman may have been persuaded by Dr. Laura's perceived feminist attitude that nothing else matters but the woman's happiness. Huh? I have never been given the impression from any feminist literature that it was okay to abandon family responsibilities for personal happiness. Personally, I think that because the traditional feminist position on abortion is pro-choice, and because Dr. Laura is so adamantly against abortion, she has simply generalized feminists as "stupid." I think she sees what she wants to see, especially if it helps cement her own views. It seems that she has targeted every negative aspect that she can find about anyone who calls herself a feminist and has assigned each aspect to the entire group. To borrow a phrase from her: How could you do that? Would that work for religion?

Let's face it, there are many people, even high-ranking leaders of various religions, who give their faith a very bad name. Some are self-centered people who take advantage of their congregations, who steal, lie and break all the commandments without remorse. Would it be fair of me to say that religion is worthless and that all religious people are just "stupid"? Would it be fair to say that there is nothing at all worthwhile about religion? I think not. Yet this is what Dr. Laura is doing with feminism. She is refusing to acknowledge anything positive about the group and the advances that have been made for women because of the actions or words of a few. Some of these words and actions are 30 years old! But she will be the first to tell you that you cannot judge a religion or the quality that it can bring to your life on the basis of the words or actions of a few who claim to subscribe.

I remember when I was a teenager and got my first driver's license. I remember how powerful it made me feel. And it truly was a new power I had never had before. I was in control more than ever before of one aspect of my life and I was free to explore the world in a whole new way. I also remember letting that feeling of power go too far by doing really irresponsible things and making very poor choices. I was recklessly *abusing* the power that I had, not paying attention to the possible consequences. After all, what could go wrong? Well, of course, things did go wrong. Nothing serious, fortunately, but enough to make me wake up and realize that new power comes with new responsibility. A fender bender and a couple of kind warnings from police officers were enough for me. I became a much more responsible driver while still in high school. But it wasn't until college and beyond that I truly took the responsibility seriously, and that was after seeing friends in devastating and even fatal accidents. Today, I drive with an entirely different perspective. In school zones and neighborhoods, I drive as though those were my children out playing. In construction zones, I drive as though that were my husband working along oncoming traffic. My change in attitude and responsibility has a lot to do with the way my views on life in general have evolved over the last 15 years. I have grown tremendously as a human being and a spiritual being. I am not at all the same person I was as a teenager. And I do not expect to be the same 15 years from now.

I can't imagine someone who knows me holding my past actions as a teenage driver against me. Yes, I let the power go to my head. Yes, I thought nothing could go wrong. But I learned from my mistakes and from the mistakes of others, and I'm a much more mature and responsible person now. I will never look that the power to drive in that way again. It's just not who I am anymore.

I want to compare this personal story to the way that, in my opinion, feminism is presented by people like Dr. Laura, Rush Limbaugh and others who use feminism as a dirty word. The introduction of the birth control pill gave

women in the '60s a new power. Women no longer needed
to avoid having sex even with their husbands for fear of an
unwanted pregnancy. It gave women the power to explore
themselves in a whole new way. Women learned new
things about how their bodies and libidos worked. They
learned that they could enjoy sex as much as men did. And
men were beneficiaries of this new freedom as women
became less inhibited about their sexuality. But, as with
any new and novel power, there was a learning curve of
responsibility. Sexually transmitted diseases increased.
Unwanted pregnancy did not disappear because the pill
was not error-proof. Women also had to learn another
lesson: sex for the sake of sex didn't pan out to be as
glamorous as it seemed from a distance.

Some women are still learning that lesson today. There
are still women trying to imitate a glamorous sexual iden-
tity. Many young women in high school and college are
trying experiment after sexual experiment. But most grown
women have come to realize that promiscuity is not a value
that they wish to carry with them or pass on to their
children.

Feminism does not stand for irresponsible sexual abandon. It really never did — that's a myth. Yes, both women
and men let the power go to their heads. Yes, they thought
that nothing could go wrong. But we learn from our
mistakes and from the mistakes of others. Feminists are a
much more mature and responsible group today. We don't
and never will look at sexual power in the same way again.
It's not who we are anymore.

Most feminists no longer see the workplace as a combat
zone, where women have to fight for every penny and shred
of recognition. We're past that now. However, we are still
pushing for equity in the workplace and in education where

it is still lacking. And it *is* still lacking in some places.

Feminists are raising their children from a new perspective as well. Our mothers have warned us about how quickly children grow up. So we have learned about priority. Working women can now scale back career goals, spend more time with their children, and then step up their careers again if they choose when their children are older. That's a fairly new concept for women. In the '70s and '80s women had to choose between a career and raising children. Many new options are available today.

And yet feminism is still bashed for the events of years past. No credit seems to be given for growth and learning. *That* gets on my nerves. Dr. Laura is still defining feminism on the basis of the "teenagers" of the '60s . It should be defined on the basis of the more mature (although still young and learning) adults. I'm asking for a little more credit, please.

When I decided to write this, I purchased Dr. Laura's latest book. I wanted her views and opinions of *today*. In fact, most of my criticisms are of things written in her latest book or said on her radio program in very recent months. I didn't want to go back to books that she had written in the past. I didn't want to criticize her for things that she may have said even four our five years ago. Why? Because that is not who she is today. May I ask the same courtesy for the feminists of today?

RELIGION

Before I get into the subject of religion, I first want to say that I respect Judaism and Christianity. I do not subscribe to either religion, and I will expand upon why I do not. My comments here are meant only as examples of why *I* have rejected these religions as a basis for *my* life. They are not at all intended to insult those who adhere to any of the faiths. I have chosen to use the term Judeo-Christianism because of the many similarities between Judaism and Christianity. The term is not meant to trivialize either belief system. So, with that caveat:

I purchased Dr. Laura's latest book, *The Ten Commandments,* because I wanted to make sure that I wouldn't mistakenly misrepresent her views on religion. As I read through it, there was so much with which I agreed and yet so much with which I disagreed and in which I still see smugness. It's mostly in the attitude: God spoke ... enough said. Black. White. Again, this is where my nerves start to frazzle.

I recently heard a caller on her show asking for advice about raising his children. My quote may not be exact word for word, but this is what I remember: Dr. Laura asked about the man's religious convictions. "I value all religions ...," he started to say. Dr. Laura immediately cut him off and replied sarcastically, "Oh! That's a great way to not commit to any; I love that cop-out." I was disgusted at her smugness. She seems to be saying on her show, as well as in her latest book, that commitment to some form of Judeo-Christianism is the only pathway to God. She says in her book, "In life, a higher idealism and a more profound, just and consistent morality is only found through the commandments."

Is *only* found? As in — *cannot be found anywhere else?*

Another recent comment made by Dr. Laura was about a woman who had written to her. The woman was commenting on a call and wrote about how she and her husband lived on $17,000 a year somewhere in Colorado. They drove old cars and made other sacrifices so that she could be at home with their two-year-old daughter. Dr. Laura went on and on about how wonderful it was that this woman was grateful for what she had and did not spend time or energy on coveting what she didn't have. That much I agree with. I agree that she is truly a special and enlightened person to have such a positive outlook on life. But then Dr. Laura went on to say that this woman "must be" a very religious person and even went on to say that the woman was "obviously" a religious person because that kind of attitude can only come from a religious background. Again, I rolled my eyes in disgust at the smugness.

Another call was from a child. I forget the topic of the conversation, but Dr. Laura was praising him for something and telling him what a remarkable young man he was. He was about 11 or 12, I think. At the end of her praising, she asked him very expectantly if his parents were religious people. She had to ask the question twice as she sort of that the Messiah has already been here and they are preparing for his return. If the Christians are right, then the Jews are wrong or vice versa. Dr. Laura has no trouble with the New Testament being optional, but the Old Testament seems mandatory. All of a sudden the black and white nature of religion is getting a little blurred as people of other religions attempt to present a united front.

When I first attended a Unity Church service, I was almost moved to tears. It was a true turning point for me. I had been focusing for years on what I *didn't* believe, dealing with the fears of letting go of traditional religious teachings. I had been thinking that I was the only one in the world who believed in God, but not necessarily in traditional religion. With the Unity Church, I could finally get down to the business of figuring out what I *did* believe. It offered me community in my search and exposure to different points of view. It offered sermons on the *connections* between the world's religions, the *similarities* more than the differences. The Unity Church in Kansas City has sponsored countless lectures and seminars by some of the world's leading-edge spiritual thinkers. It truly opened a door for me.

I was amazed and immediately at home in the Unity Church. I met people who had been asking the same types of questions that I had been asking. It was wonderful to be in an atmosphere where I felt that I could pose the questions and even share my nontraditional point of view without being told that I was wrong. I could participate in debates without being told that if I would just open my heart to Jesus or to the Bible or to God, all of my questions would just disappear. I was once told that my questions about God were blasphemy in and of themselves. God was God — He could do anything, whether or not it made sense to me. After all, who was I to doubt God's greatness? Who was I to question God's motives? That's nonsense. Opening my heart does not mean that I close my mind!

If God was truly the being that traditional religions describe, could He really be so egotistical and insecure that He couldn't handle a few logical questions born of the rational mind that He gave me? Even Dr. Laura describes God in the traditional Judeo-Christian image of being a benevolent yet sometimes ill-tempered old man. I was pleased to see her state that "God is greater than form and beyond our sensory abilities." At one point she describes God as being like "the Force" in the *Star Wars* movies. I like that metaphor and agree completely. I believe that human beings have absolutely no concept in our five-sensory world of what God is and is not. But no matter how much Judeo-Christian religions give lip service to that idea, and no matter that they claim that to do so is idolatry, all of them, in my opinion, fall back on attributing human characteristics to God. Even according to Dr. Laura, God demands, God gets disappointed, God cherishes, God loves, God hates and God talked openly with Biblical people. God defines good and bad, God gives gifts, God makes promises, God gets offended, God is vengeful, God can be pleased or displeased, God suffers, God even tells white lies. And if we're not careful, God is easily confused: Dr. Laura writes, "According to Jewish tradition, if someone is approaching home and sees a fire from the distance, he or she may *not* say, 'God, please let this not be my house.' Such a prayer could be misinterpreted as a plea that it be someone else's house." This seems a bit odd for an omnipotent being.

A good friend of mine, Mike Lombardi, summarized his views of the inconsistencies of Judeo-Christian religions this way:

1. *God is perfect and all-knowing and all-loving.*

2. *God wants company (but doesn't really need it-see #1).*

3. *God creates Lucifer and angels. He didn't really need them. These rebel.*

4. *God knew they would rebel and evil would be introduced into the world (see #1). God should therefore be accountable for creating evil, but we let him off the hook on this one because, after all, it wasn't Him but those free willed creations of His. (So, tell me, who created these uncontrollable free willed creatures in the first place, huh?)*

5. *God creates humans.*

6. *Humans are a disappointment, they sin, partly due to temptation from Satan, that earlier creation of God's.*

7. *God knew this would happen (see #1).*

8. *Because God is so fair, the transgression of Adam and Eve and its punishment is visited upon not only them but also all their descendants, who incidentally had nothing to do with the eating of the forbidden fruit (review #1).*

9. *After a while, God regrets he created man (see #1) and sends a huge flood to destroy all but Noah and family, making Him the greatest premeditated mass murderer of men, women, and children in history (see #1).*

10. *Throughout the Old Testament, this perfect being needs*

rest, gets jealous, becomes angry, demands sacrifices, and commands the total destruction of neighboring tribes. He invites Satan to heaven (How come he gets visiting rights? — see #1), makes a bet and then abandons Job to the most miserable treatment just to prove a point . Yes, he restores Job's wealth and gives him new children but that's like saying if I kill your grown son and give you a new baby, you should not feel you've lost anything.

11. *God gives the "gift" of eternal life, but only to those who are willing to accept it in the spirit in which it is given. To those who don't accept, He doesn't just leave them alone to live out their earthly existence; not quite- he's not done- He gives them eternal life but with a twist- eternal torment (see #1). From the parable of Lazarus, we should surmise that those who make it to heaven will live in uninterrupted bliss all the while being within eternal earshot of screams from those family members and friends in Hell who didn't quite make it.*

12. *We come to the modern age with its multiplicity of religions and bizarre beliefs, each claiming to be the only true path and all others are false, leading to damnation.*

Does this all hang together? I doubt it.

Does God show evidence of being an ineffective chief executive? Like a poor manager, He does not make a real effort to properly communicate his message (He could use modern broadcast media if He wanted to), doesn't tell you His message directly but prefers to deal indirectly (through prophets and assorted others). He communicates in coded messages, hard to figure out, and does so very infrequently (He stopped saying much about 2000 years ago). He gets

will purge himself of pride that he is "not as other men." Then, and only then, may he reach for the feet of those who do not fear contamination from his grubby hands. To expand the heart to Oneness, and beyond, such is the meaning of Enlightenment, for the Buddha-Mind is one with the Universe, one with the All-Mind from which it came.

The meaning behind the presence of evil is a question that most religions must attempt to answer. It is also another question that Judeo-Christianism answers inadequately for me. The notion that there is yet another being, separate from ourselves, rejoicing in evil and trying to *win souls* away from God by perpetrating evil, makes no sense to me. I view "evil" as a tool of the soul, a learning experience, for the perpetrator as well as the victim(s). Although the lessons can be incomprehensible to the human mind, especially to the victim, I believe that they become clear to the soul and contribute to its growth. A belief in karma is essential here. However, this is not unlike the Judeo-Christian belief that God has some purpose behind why bad things happen to good people and that He ultimately judges and punishes the evildoers.

Some people look at me like I'm nuts when I try to describe my view of God and the Universe. But it really isn't much different from any religious viewpoint. For example, to pray to God, in my opinion, is to meditate and make a connection through the soul to the greater collective. It's a dose of spiritual energy.

Jews and Christians believe that prayer is a way of making a connection to God; I agree. Jews and Christians believe that the soul is immortal; I agree. Jews and Christians believe that God is a force in their lives that can lead them to be better human beings; I agree. Dr. Laura writes that "Scriptures clarify God's will for our behaviors"; I agree that they can. So can Gary Zukov's book, *The Seat of the Soul*. Speaking of that book, I highly recommend it to anyone who is relating to what I'm saying here. Zukov's explanations and summaries of the concepts of karma, intent, evolution and power are truly inspiring.

Dr. Laura writes that "the Ten Commandments seem like an excellent formula for making one a 'better person'." I agree with that also. But then, I like the Buddhist eight-fold path as well; it's even more compelling, in my opinion. Right Mindfulness — now *that's* an enlightening spiritual challenge!

Dr. Laura has spoken and written about the many virtues of religious rituals. She writes, "Without these reminders we can too easily become crass and self-centered." I have a couple of problems with this. The first is simply that rituals do not have the same effect on each of us. For some people like Dr. Laura, rituals offer a spiritual connection. They can have an elevating effect.

But this is not true for all people or all the time. For some people, rituals tend to lose meaning as they are repeated. This does not mean that the person is losing his connection, only that he should probably find a different way to express it. I know people who almost never go to church, never pray in the traditional sense or light candles on the proper holidays. But these same people are known to be kind and loving people. They are some of the most generous and compassionate people whom I know. They have no trouble making spiritual connections with the Divine.

Again, if religious rituals make you feel closer to God, I'm happy for you. But do not insist that a lack of observing rituals is an indication of a lack of spirituality.

Speaking of rituals leads me to my second point. Many religious people, Dr. Laura included, hold the smug attitude that *their* rituals are serious and pious and that everyone else's are trash. Dr. Laura writes, "All the serious rituals and customs that bring a true understanding of God and lead us to living sacred lives are cheapened by putting superstitions on par with religious observances." Now, who put *her* in charge of deciding the difference between spirituality and superstition?

I guess that some would consider me a somewhat super-stitious person, even though I don't avoid black cats, or stay in on Friday the 13th. But, in keeping with my view of the Universe and how I believe that it works, I do respect the spiritual energy that may be present anywhere at any time.

Here's yet another personal story: My husband and I painted the first house we bought. We had purchased the house from its original owner, who had lived there for over 40 years. Inside the hall closet door were pencil marks showing the growth of her son whom she had raised in that house and also of her grandson, both of whom are adults now. I chose not to paint over those marks. I viewed them as a part of the spiritual presence of the house. To have scraped them off and covered them over would, in my opinion, have been to slight that spirit somehow. Maybe it was silly, but I felt very strongly about it, and it did not cheapen my spirituality. In fact, to have ignored my intu-ition would have been to diminish my belief system.

Unfortunately, this notion that *our rituals are sacred, yours are superstitions* or *our stories are God's Word, yours are silly myths* permeates Judeo-Christianism. So also does the notion that it's okay to act immorally as long as you can find some justification in the Bible.

Slavery, for example, is not a spiritually healthy institution in any form. But Dr. Laura finds justification: "The Hebrew Bible, with its strict, protective laws about servants (slaves), is the first document to give rights and privileges to those slaves; a fact that many theologians believe was to set in place slavery's ultimate abolishment." It's interesting to me that she wants to give Judaism some credit for the eventual abolishment.

Another example is the rationalization of war. This one is especially interesting because, again, we have the notion of *when others do it, it's merciless mayhem, but when we do it, it's okay.* Why? *Because God said so.* Dr. Laura writes, "Though there are too many religious factions declaring so-called 'holy wars' to justify their barbarous, immoral actions, there is such a thing as a moral, obligatory war." Oh yeah? Like when? When would be a logical time for God to set aside the Sixth Commandment and say, "Ya know what? I'm in the mood for some blood and guts!" This is one of the places where religion (not just its followers) gets a reputation for being hypocritical.

Dr. Laura goes on to say, "Although war is sometimes a necessary evil, the worst thing that might happen to us is that we become arrogant, insensitive, without compassion or pity. That is why civilized countries have rules of war and demand justice for war crimes." Civilized countries? If we're so civilized, how come we haven't come up with a better way to settle our differences?

Self-defense or the protection of another country can force us into war, but that still does not make war a moral action. Has it occurred to anyone else that we are supposed to be learning and figuring out a way to avoid killing each other that way?

Where I think that I have an advantage over Judeo-

Christianism is in the processing of new information. When Biblical scholars find historical inaccuracies and inconsistencies in the Bible, I do not have to reject their findings for fear of offending God. When scholars of the Aramaic language report that the first few books of the New Testament were written 200 or more years after the death of Jesus, and that even their words were poorly translated and their message distorted, I do not have to believe that Satan is at work in their minds. The concept of life on other planets does not upset my vision of the Universe or of God. I can appreciate the spiritual offerings of just about any and every culture, religion or spiritual belief system because I can see the similarities without getting offended by the differing symbols and rituals.

I suppose the main reason that I have not committed myself to any one particular religion is because each religion has its own exclusive set of core beliefs about the nature of God and the Universe. Each generally draws the same conclusions about the meaning of life and offers similar suggestions about how we should interact with each other and with the rest of the planet. But each has an explanation of events and a perspective of God that excludes other logical points of view. Complete commitment to one particular religion generally involves a complete rejection of all other religions and belief systems.

Buddhists believe that our souls incarnate many times as human beings. I think that may be true for some souls, but not necessarily always true. Followers of the Bahai faith believe that each of the major religious figures, Jesus, Buddha, Mohammed, etc. had the spiritual message and guidance for his place and time. That makes sense to me. But they also believe that Bahaullah is the messenger for this time; I'm not convinced about that. Christians believe that Jesus Christ was the Son of God; I agree with that, but only insofar as I believe that we are *all* children of God.

This religious exclusiveness, especially in the Judeo-Christian religions, is apparent in the views of Dr. Laura when she writes: "Primitive cultures actually worshipped nature directly. This, of course, was man's attempt to control nature." I could not disagree more with this statement. It is evidence to me of a complete lack of understanding as well as an unwillingness to understand. Dr. Laura does not mention specifically to which cultures she is referring, so we have to guess. Pagan? How about Native American? It could be any one of many cultures. I believe that these "primitive" cultures were not worshipping nature; they were worshipping *God* as evidenced *by and through* nature. Can you see the difference? Earthquakes and floods were not gods to be worshipped. They were reminders of the power of God. A drought or a tornado could destroy life in the physical realm, so primitive cultures' faith was centered on the greater plan of God or of the Universe or whatever word you want to use.

Many of the Native American cultures had a greater appreciation of nature than did the Europeans who took over this country because they believed that they were as much an integral part of the Earth as each and every other living being. It is the Judeo-Christian religions that teach that God gave man dominion over the rest of life on Earth, and that man was God's greatest creation. What an ego trip! Other more "primitive" cultures taught that *life* was to be valued — all life — and that greater intelligence did not bequeath human life with more value in God's plan.

I believe this to be true: life is life — in any form; it is all *of God.* And so I have rejected the notion of man's superiority on Earth. One need simply look at what we've done with our supposed intelligence and rank. We have yet to learn to coexist peacefully. We have destroyed and depleted natural resources and hunted or displaced animals to near extinction. Somehow I just don't think that's what God had in mind.

Another example of the similarities of the world's religions comes again from Mike Lombardi. I particularly like this one because of the tie-in to mathematics:

I think we can tie in the "Bible is metaphor" idea, religion, atheism, and mathematics all in one. Here we go ...

If you had a specific problem bothering you, for example the equation 2x + 8 = 0, you would no doubt eventually say you have the answer and the answer is x=-8/2 or simplifying x =-4. A different person would be struggling with a similar problem, say 5x -10=0, and conclude, "no, the answer is x=10/5 or simplifying x=2."

Before long, a math teacher would come along and point out that the reason for the multiplicity of similar problems and apparently different solutions is because the issue is being framed too narrowly. They actually all have a common element. They could be generalized into the broader algebraic form Ax + B = 0 and the common solution is x= -B/A.

Now back to religion. Jews and Christians clearly have a specific view of the world and the purpose of life, with a single solution that works for them. Fine, but then they condemn the rest of us for not seeing the same problem and/or not agreeing to their solution. Their blissful happiness in having discovered "the answer" seems to make them too ready to reject all other approaches, sometimes very forcefully so.

Let's generalize for a second. We really all do have the same problem and consistent solutions. If we broaden the definitions as follows:

A is "that which we seek as our goal in life, that which gives our life meaning."

B is "the consequence of failing to achieve our goal in life."

C is "that which we rely on to guide our behavior and thinking."

D is "the abstract force which guides us to the answer."

Then we can frame everyone's different views in a similar light.

For a Christian A=Eternal life, B=Hell, C=the Bible, and D=Jesus Christ.

For a Jew, perhaps A=Eternal life, B=Hell, C=the Old Testament and Talmud, and D=God.

For a more liberal minded religious individual A= being forever in God's presence, B= eternal absence from God, C and D could vary broadly.

Now if we generalize a bit further to include those who believe in reincarnation: A=to learn from our past lives and advance the soul to greater perfection, B= failing to advance to the next step, C and D would be the needs of our soul, that which we seek.

Finally, to generalize further to those who doubt spirituality of any kind, an atheist like Bertrand Russell might say, A= the advancement of human achievement, knowledge, and compassion, B=continuing with fear, superstition, and needless suffering, making life a mockery of what it ought to be , C=the lessons of history and D =science, logic and reason.

Conclusion: We all seek to achieve our purpose in life (call it fulfilling our particular view of God's will) in the manner we feel most comfortable and consistent with our beliefs. It reminds me of a story of a son asking his father "Dad, tell me what did you really want me to grow up to become? A doctor? A lawyer? A teacher? Are you happy with my choice?" And the father replies "Why, nothing very specific, I am just pleased to see you happy, using your talents to their fullest, and being the best at that you can be."

Perhaps, if we can imagine asking God a similar question: "What did you really want me to believe? Christianity? Judaism? Islam ...?" We may find a broad-minded God giving a similar reply. Instead of there being but one narrow track, the many supposed paths to truth may actually converge.

Since I was not able to come up with an existing religion that I could agree with on the structural points, I have chosen to appreciate all but subscribe to none. Some people, including, I think, Dr. Laura, would then conclude that I am left without a spiritual foundation. This is not so. I am clear on my perspective about God, about how the Universe works, and about what I believe the meaning of human life to be. My belief system is not subject to change according to my whims or according to the way that I would like things to be. It does not alleviate personal responsibility or remove accountability. I have a clear understanding of my obligations to God and to the people and other beings in my life. It is this foundation upon which the rest of my spiritual and moral structure rests. What more could one ask for in a religion besides a nice building and a set of holidays?

MARRIAGE, LIVING TOGETHER AND SEX

MOST OF THE DISAGREEMENTS that I have with Dr. Laura are due to our differing views on life in general. This results in our different perspectives on the meaning of life and our obligations and responsibilities to ourselves, to others and to God.

Keep in mind that when I use the word God, I am referring to the abstract concept as described in the chapter on religion. In theory, this concept is not much different from the way Dr. Laura describes it. It refers to the Divine, the Universe, the Power, the "Force," whatever you want to call it. But because I conceptualize God differently than Dr. Laura does, my views are not restricted to the Biblical concept of God.

As I tried to explain in the preceding chapter, I believe that our experiences as human beings are opportunities for our souls to grow and learn and also to connect. As humans, our personalities are shaped by our fears, our desires and our capacity for love and compassion. We acquire these attributes in differing degrees and varieties by virtue of the environment in which we are raised. As we grow into adults, these traits are molded and honed by our childhood experiences. By early adulthood, most of us are sporting a pretty broad ensemble of fears, desires and capacities for love and compassion.

I believe that each individual's soul comes into this life by Divine choice, much like Judeo-Christian religions teach. But contrary to the religious traditions, I believe that the set of physical circumstances is chosen by each soul for a reason. Each soul has its lessons to be learned and its work to be done. I believe that fear is a huge obstacle to enlightenment (or heaven, or eternal connection to God, or whatever). I believe that by incarnating as human beings and learning to overcome fears, our souls make tremendous progress toward enlightenment. Tremendous advances are also made by the lessons learned about love and compassion.

So, what does all this have to do with sex?

There is rarely a greater state of vulnerability for a human being than that which sex yields. Other animals of the world have sex for procreation and do so shamelessly. Humans, on the other hand, have sex for a multitude of other reasons. Sometimes we have sex to show affection to someone else. But mostly we just do it for self-centered reasons. Even when we are making others and even ourselves believe that we're not being self-centered when it comes to sex, most of the time we are.

Sometimes we are working through our fears of intimacy. We can fool ourselves into thinking that we're not afraid of being close, and yet we will hide behind the sex of uncommitted relationships. Sometimes we are insecure about ourselves. I believe that the reason that many teenage girls have sex is because they are looking for validation that they are attractive and sexy. Our society places tremendous value on *looking sexy*. I don't need to go into the many examples of that. Many girls have sex as a way to feel

where the partners genuinely want and promote what is best for themselves, as individuals and as part of the partnership.

For most religious people, a healthy "holy" intimate relationship is founded on marriage vows between a man and a woman. Dr. Laura writes, "Holy sex is that which takes place between a husband and wife in fulfillment of their marital relationship. Unholy sex is everything else." Black. White. Personally, I think that there are just too many gray areas where sex is concerned. And there are lessons to be learned in a variety of circumstances.

Dr. Laura also writes, "People are shacking up instead of marrying because they can't see that there is any difference in outcome between a covenant before God and an agreement to cohabit as long as it seems satisfying." Huh? Of course there is a difference! That's why so many people do it!

On the surface, I think that many people choose to cohabit *because* the commitment is less binding. They have learned from the examples set by others or even from their own experiences that divorces can be messy. They do not want to get involved in a legally binding contract just yet — or maybe never. This does not mean that they are not learning and growing as individuals. This does not mean that they are not capable of commitment. It doesn't even mean they aren't *willing* to commit to marriage. But there can be so much to learn. Often people can and do choose to learn about themselves in relationships without commitment. People can learn quite a lot about commitment by *not* having one, just as they can by having one. Then once the lessons are learned, lack of a legal commitment makes it easier to move on.

I once joked to the disgust of a conservative Christian friend that people should be required to have sex with at least five different partners before being allowed to marry. I was kidding, of course, but in all seriousness, I would recommend it. I think it is in our sexual relationships that we learn the most about ourselves. Some of the lessons are easy and short-lived, but, again, some come with consequences. We learn about our bodies, what pleases us and what pleases our partner. We learn not only about physical pleasures but also about how we treat others and want to be treated emotionally. We learn about our insecurities. We learn about jealousy and envy. We learn whether we are ready to become committed to another person for the rest of our lives by the way we interact with them at each other's most vulnerable moments.

Sometimes it is better to learn some of the lessons through relationships with partners other than a spouse. Once the marriage commitment is made, it is often too late. Many people simply put aside certain aspects of themselves once they are married because there is too much at stake. They do not want to risk exploring another side of themselves with someone who now has expectations of them in a marriage. Or worse, sometimes characteristics surface in marriage that were hidden during dating. Often these symptoms are simply ignored, but it is certainly easier to hide certain traits in a dating situation than it is in a cohabiting or marriage situation.

I know that many people, especially religious people, disagree with me, but I simply cannot imagine marrying someone and not knowing what to expect sexually. I've known a few people (not many, but a few) who were virgins on their wedding nights. None has recommended it to me. Most have described their first experience as awkward, even disappointing. All have said that there were aspects of their spouse's personality that they were not aware of prior to the commencement of the sexual relationship.

Advocates of waiting for the wedding night extol the benefits of the element of surprise. They claim that any sexual problems or incompatibilities can be worked out in the normal course of a "holy" marriage. Most people today who are making a serious commitment to marriage prefer to have all of the cards on the table ahead of time. I believe that this would be the most beneficial route to take — but only if people *would* be willing to work through their sexual "issues" before marriage.

Trouble is, people think that they've learned enough about themselves — when they haven't. The number of partners is not really the key here. The key is putting the effort into learning and growing. Having an intimate sexual relationship with another person provides an *opportunity* for learning; it does not guarantee that we will learn.

I should mention in all of this that I do believe that children should not be brought into the picture outside of a committed marriage. I say this because I agree with Dr. Laura that it is best for children to be raised in a two-parent home where they (hopefully) have the opportunity to witness a loving relationship between two people. I also say this because I cannot imagine how single parents raise children! I am in awe of single parents who can maintain loving and nurturing relationships with their children. I have a difficult enough time with just one child and a husband who's a saint!

Some people might say that my views on sex are nothing more than a way to rationalize immoral behavior. It might appear that as long as a person says "I'm learning about myself," it's okay to be promiscuous. I can see where that misunderstanding would occur. But it's not up to me to set the curriculum for another person. It's not up to me to decide the best way for another person to learn about himself. I can have compassion for a person as he struggles to learn that only by giving of himself will he find true love. I can even have sympathy for a person as she learns that love itself is not enough to sustain a relationship, much less a marriage. But ultimately each person's struggles and lessons are his own. It makes no difference how I see them. Therefore, it is useless for me to spend time or energy deciding whether they are "right" or "wrong."

What I can do is learn from observing others' struggles. It's even possible to do this by watching television or movies. I am amused when I hear people like Dr. Laura lamenting about how television and movies glamorize sex. She quotes Barbara Bartocci of *Women's Day* magazine: "When we romanticize adultery or use it as a slapstick tool to provoke laughter — as if the hurt and betrayal are inconsequential — what kind of values are we teaching?" The problem is that she's not paying enough attention. Last year I heard Dr. Laura talking about the movie *My Best Friend's Wedding*. She was saying that she had refused to see the movie, if I remember correctly. Another listener (I don't recall whether it was a caller or a fax) was backing her up by saying that she had walked out of the theater because of the way Julia Roberts' character was being portrayed. The movie seemed to be saying that it was okay to try to break up a friend's wedding and steal the groom away just because she was beautiful and because she wanted him for herself. Dr. Laura chimed right in, remember not having not seen the movie, and proclaimed that she refused to watch such movies. I just had to laugh. Too bad really, because the point was missed entirely by both Dr. Laura and the listener.

The person who had walked out missed the end — the

part where Roberts' character realizes that she has acted selfishly. The climax of the film occurs when she goes to great lengths to set everything right again just before the wedding and apologizes in a toast to the bride and groom. Oh, what a horrible concept!

Television shows also may often appear to people like Dr. Laura to be attempting to legitimize promiscuity, but I choose to look a little closer. I pay attention to what happens to the characters after the sex is over. Usually, they learn something. Sometimes it's not very direct. But when they go on to experience the consequences, it's an opportunity for viewers to learn, even if the characters do not seem to "get it." You just have to be willing to look a little deeper, I suppose.

On her show, Dr. Laura has blamed teenagers having sex on a lack of parental authority and a void of strength in teens. It would be nice if it were that simple. People who would like to think so are raising their children with very strict guidelines. Now, I have nothing against setting boundaries and teaching morality to teenagers, but it seems to me that most parents who do this believe that it's enough and assume that their children are therefore not having sex. Unfortunately, what is happening more often than not is that the children of these parents are in fact having sex; they are just taking great care not to let their parents know. I knew parents when I was a teenager who basically told their children that sex was off-limits, period. They would then brag to their friends about how easy it was to raise teenagers, so long as rules were set. What they didn't know was that these kids were going to Planned Parenthood and having sex anyway. The sad part was when it came time for the inevitable lessons. These kids had nowhere to turn. They could not go to their parents and explain that they were pregnant or needed to see a doctor. They simply had to deal with the consequences on their own. I even knew parents who said to their children, *If you get pregnant or get a disease, you may as well not come home.* What they thought they were doing was instilling such fear into their kids that the kids would avoid sex. What happened was that the kids simply learned to avoid their parents.

Lest you start thinking that I'm not talking about your kid, I want to mention that I'm not just talking about weak kids from broken homes or kids with no parental guidance or kids with disinterested parents. I was a pretty good student in school, so most of my friends were at the top of the academic ladder. These were intelligent and educated kids. Their parents were well-respected leaders in the community. Their parents were the type of people who call into Dr. Laura and proclaim, "I'm my kids' mom!" And they meant well and tried hard. And their children still had sex.

My parents took a different and controversial approach. Late in my teens, my mother allowed me to purchase birth control pills. She took me to a doctor who spoke to me openly about how to protect myself and also about the advantages of not having sex at all. Many parents believe that this approach tells teens that it's okay to have sex. And it probably isn't the right approach for all kids. But for me it worked well. What it told me was that my parents wanted to protect me, because they loved me. But it also told me that they trusted my judgment. They knew that they could not supervise my every moment, and they knew that I was strong-willed enough that I would make up my own mind about sex when I thought I was ready. Knowing that they trusted me instilled more responsibility in me than a strict set of rules would have done.

I think that this is especially true for today's parents,

that which should or will become reality. In the proper context and between loving and secure partners, fantasies can be simply an enjoyable diversion.

Another concept with which Dr. Laura seems to take issue is that of platonic friendships among married people. I have heard a number of callers ask, *What should I do? We've been friends for years, it's strictly platonic, but my spouse is giving me grief.* Dr. Laura's answer is simple: Choose between your friend or your spouse — and you had better choose your spouse, the logic being that within a marriage, you should do nothing to undermine the security of the other partner.

I can agree with that to a certain extent. However, I'm always curious (and Dr. Laura doesn't ask) about how many other aspects of the caller's life that his or her spouse is trying to control. Does he accuse you of having an affair with the waiter who smiled at you at dinner? Does she insist on chaperoning you while you go to put gas in your car? This is kind of important. Also, have you given any *reason* for your spouse to be insecure? When the insecurity is unfounded or just plain ridiculous, there is much more to be dealt with than the single platonic friend. But Dr. Laura never seems to go there.

Similarly, I remember a call from a young woman whose boyfriend was insisting that she give up drinking. The young woman seemed to know that this was a control issue and tried to bring this into the discussion, but Dr. Laura cut her off and simply told her to choose between her boyfriend and alcohol, the implication being that she probably had a drinking problem. What was never asked was how much and how often she took a drink. If she were boozing it up on a regular basis, that would be one thing. Her boyfriend would have had cause to be concerned about her. If she was merely enjoying an occasional glass of wine in a social setting, then that's another. Then it becomes a control issue. Personally, I enjoy a margarita now and then. I view it much the way that I view a hot fudge sundae. It's something I could do without, but I really enjoy the taste. So occasionally I indulge in one. If a boyfriend ever insisted that I give that up, you can bet which one I would choose!

Masturbation is another topic that Dr. Laura mentions briefly in her book. I've not heard her discuss it on her radio show, and she speaks of it only in the context of masturbating while looking at pornography, so I wasn't quite sure if it was the act of self-gratification or pornography or both that she was against. My guess is both. She writes: "Some folks, generally men, will spend an inordinate amount of time masturbating over photos and videos. This form of sexuality is devoid of sanctity, true feeling, and a relationship to another person or anything divine."

As far as masturbation is concerned, I can only say that I would wonder about any person, male or female, who is so intimidated by his or her own sexuality that he or she is unable to touch his or her own body and experience the pleasure of it. Of course it is devoid of a relationship — that's the point. It's not supposed to be sacred or divine. It is simply a physical and private release. Incidentally, as most teenagers try it out, masturbation can be a way of exploring one's own body without actually having intercourse. It also offers a release for those sexual fantasies, that we're not supposed to have — even though everybody does.

What about adultery?

I have a conservative Christian friend who confided in

ABORTION

IF YOU LISTEN to Dr. Laura's radio show for any length of time, you will hear her views on abortion. It is clear that she views it as an immoral act. She often uses graphic phrases such as "sucked into a sink." Now, I've never heard her suggest that the practice should be illegal. I'm glad about that. To me, the moral issue is quite separate from the legal issue. So I'm happy to see her at least stick to the moral side of things.

However, as you might have guessed, I still have a few problems with her absolutist and, in my opinion, smug moral stance. I take issue with the inconsistency of her stand on abortion alone and also when it is compared to other forms of ending human life.

Let's start with the stand-alone issue. In her book, Dr. Laura writes, "[The fetus] is considered a potential life — not to be terminated without sufficient cause." Sufficient cause being the "mother's life or sanity." Bad timing or the wrong guy, she declares, "trivialize the blessing and miracle of life." So it's okay to have an abortion, so long as the criteria for the decision fit into Dr. Laura's moral framework. The problem that I have with this is that, again, her moral framework is presented as the only acceptable structure. If one does not view abortion in the same light, she is branded by Dr. Laura as self-centered, narcissistic and uncaring. Many times I've heard her paste these labels on women on her show. Often it's when she's talking to a caller about someone else. Dr. Laura and the caller, neither of whom have all of the information, bash the other woman who's had or is thinking of having an abortion. Can you imagine sharing your reasons for considering an abortion with a so-called friend whom you know would not agree with you? I can't. But that doesn't stop Dr. Laura.

Once I heard her talking to a woman who was contemplating having an abortion instead of giving up the child for adoption. The woman was concerned that once she had the baby she would not be able to let it go, even though her circumstances were not ideal for raising a baby. Dr. Laura came back sarcastically with: "So you could kill it, but you can't wave bye-bye? You're an interesting mother!" I find that comment absolutely disgusting. I have known a dozen or more women who have had abortions. In all cases, they had them when they were not in an ideal situation to raise a baby because of "bad timing" and /or "the wrong guy." Almost all of these woman are now mothers. And they are wonderful mothers. All of them have said that there was no comparison between the two pregnancy situations. One was clearly a scary and sobering situation to be corrected and the other was absolute euphoria. Each has also expressed some regret, not necessarily for the abortion itself, but, again, for not being wiser to begin with. None would go back and change their decision now.

There is a tremendous difference between how a woman feels when she is presented with the lesson of an unwanted pregnancy and how she feels when she is about to become believe that God has ordered them to war. I have never found much logic in the above rationalizations. But then, as Dr. Laura herself writes, "Human beings can rationalize anything as okay if it's something they desire to possess or to do without consequences."

Capital punishment is clearly the taking of a living, breathing, viable human life. And, in some cases, the person dying is in fact innocent. The judicial system is not perfect, after all. But that is the price that some people believe we should be willing to pay for the chance to kill violent criminals. However, when it comes to abortion, many of these same people do not believe that an unwanted, nonviable fetus should be terminated. Many of these same people do not believe that a terminally ill person, living in pain, should be allowed to die peacefully. The argument that Dr. Laura uses is this: "The simple fact is that it is not for us to play God by deciding when someone's time is up."

And yet she apparently has no problem making the *time's up* decision for a criminal. She seems to have no problem with military leaders making that decision — provided, of course, that the war is "moral" and "obligatory." I find these positions on capital punishment and war to be completely at odds with the opinions on abortion and euthanasia.

Of course, I like to think that my position on all four issues is much more logical and consistent. As I said before, I believe that life is life. Since I believe that we are all directly connected to the Divine, it follows that we are all directly connected to each other. Likewise, we are connected to all other life forms. Dr. Laura acknowledges and I agree that "God's law reminds us that no one is to be valued less than ourselves." I would even extend that to include all other forms of life — animals and even plants. I am not of the opinion that humans have been given dominion over all other forms of life. I believe that all life is *of God* — it has all been created *in His image*.

That said, in order to sustain life, we must sometimes take the life of other beings. We must consume other plants and animals in order to survive. We have taken the lives of animals in order to keep warm and even to use for fuel for our survival (although that is no longer necessary). I believe that capital punishment can be viewed as a necessary means to keeping social order. Practical problems arise when the system of justice is imperfect, but, in theory, I think that capital punishment is morally justifiable.

War is difficult to justify, in my opinion. There are times, I suppose, when it becomes inevitable. I do not hold individuals accountable for the actual killing that occurs in war. But I do hold the military leadership of a group responsible. Again, it simply seems to me that with our supposed superior intelligence, we ought to have come up with a better way.

Euthanasia, in my opinion, is simply no one else's business. I believe that the soul is a completely separate entity from the human body. The soul is immortal and can never be extinguished. The human body, however, is a very fragile being. When someone is overcome with disease and/or pain, I do not believe that letting go of the body (or even assisting someone in that process) is an immoral act.

Likewise, again, since the soul is separate from the body, abortion in most cases does not pose a moral problem. I do not believe that most women who have abortions have a disregard for human life. On the contrary, the women I have known who have terminated pregnancies

MOTHERING — AND THE CHILD CARE ISSUE

LATELY DR. LAURA has been making a smug comparison on the issue of child day care. She wonders how many women who put their children in day care would be okay with a prostitute in the bedroom with their husbands. According to her, it's the same thing. You wouldn't want a prostitute substituting for you in the bedroom, so how can you allow someone else to substitute for you as a mother? She has made this comparison a number of times on her radio show, and each time I am torn between disgust and amusement. This smug comparison is meant to make mothers who have career interests feel guilty for every moment spent away from their children. I think that Dr. Laura would agree with me as to the intent of that statement.

Each time that I hear child care providers compared to prostitutes, I think to myself, *Well, I wouldn't want another woman sleeping with my husband any more than I would want my child's babysitter to breastfeed her!* I have allowed other people to change her diaper, give her a bottle and play with her. And I would be more than happy to allow any other woman to come to my home and do my husband's laundry or cook a meal! He is often entertained by other people, but he doesn't have sex with them. Babysitters don't snuggle up with my baby at night either.

In her book, Dr. Laura proclaims that, "Having children virtually from birth taken care of by strangers robs them of their early, and necessary, experience with loving, attentive parents, and steals their innocence." And yet in another section she states that, "According to Jewish tradition, anyone who teaches a child is considered to be like a parent and accorded the same respect." Hmmm. Now which is it?

First of all, we should define the word "stranger." I have never known any mother who has ever left her children with a stranger. We're drifting into that straw-man area of argument at which Dr. Laura is so proficient. I do know mothers who work. Each of them spent months searching and interviewing, looking for the best child care that they could find. Often the caregivers are relatives or friends, but I have never known them to be strangers. Even in the case of a day care center, where the caregivers may be new to the child, how long must you know someone before they lose the title of Stranger? My guess is long before one's innocence is stolen!

Next we must make a distinction between parents who *have to* work and parents who *choose to* work. Recently I heard Dr. Laura on the radio belittling an advertisement she had seen. It was for some sort of product designed to help working parents, specifically those in the business world. One of the lines in the ad went something like, "Since parents in business rarely spend as much time with their children as they would like." The product was supposed to give parents ideas about how to make their time with their children more special. It offered stories to be shared or something like that. Anyway, when Dr. Laura read the part about parents rarely spending as much time as they would like with their children, she interjected that the notion was complete nonsense. "It's all choice," she stated more than once. She insisted that parents could have all the time in the world if they would only choose to spend it with their children. My first thought was, *Gee, don't most kids like to eat?* Even if one parent is at home full-time, isn't it feasible that the other parent is probably out earning a living? Wouldn't it then follow that the working parent might miss the children?

I do agree with Dr. Laura that it is too easily assumed in our society that both parents must work full-time in order to support a family. I agree that in most cases, with a little effort and sacrifice, one parent could stay home. However, there are about as many different sets of circumstances for today's families as there are families!

I suppose that I would have to agree that the Cleaver family seemed to have it all together: the stay-at-home mom, the working dad and two delightful precocious children. But, not all moms are June Cleaver. And I don't really think all moms *need* to be or should even *try* to be June Cleaver. I know lots of people who have children. In some cases, the mom is at home. In some cases, the dad is at home. In some cases, both parents work. Sometimes one parent works from home. Sometimes one parent works just part-time. Sometimes, both parents work full-time.

I have inferred from listening to Dr. Laura that she believes that the only acceptable way to raise children is for one parent to be at home at all times, preferably the mother during the first year of each child's life. Working is acceptable only while the children are in school and then at least one parent must be home after school. I think that Dr. Laura would agree that I've summarized her position.

Recently a woman called her show. She was an attorney and she and her husband were expecting their first child. She wanted to know if Dr. Laura would approve of her working two days a week after her maternity leave was over. *Absolutely not,* came the answer. Even if the sitter was a relative? *Even if.* Another woman caller wanted to know if Dr. Laura would accept as satisfactory a sitter for her eight-month-old for just two *mornings* a week. *Absolutely not,* came the answer.

I appreciate the push for a return to the days of stay-at-home parents. But two days a week? As I said, I know many families in all types of situations. All are raising wonderful children. Some are struggling, but the struggles seem to be pretty much universal. Even the families in which both parents work full-time seem to me to be doing just fine. Personally, I chose not to return to full-time employment after my daughter was born. I initially returned on a three-days-per-week schedule. My daughter was with her grandmother for those three days and she did just fine. Even at four months old, she was perfectly capable of distinguishing me from anyone else, and she had no trouble making the transition. In fact, even though Dr. Laura may disagree, I think that the time spent away from me had its benefits. I have never been as adept as I'd like to be at providing good stimulation to babies. Other people are better at it than me. Does that make me a bad mother? I don't think so. And since, like any mother, I want what is best for my child, I sometimes think that it benefits her to be around other people.

Some other mothers I know have admitted to enjoying their careers more than changing diapers and playing airplane-spoon with cereal. Does this mean that they don't love their children? I don't think so. Does it mean that they don't have their priorities straight? I don't think so. I don't know any working mother who does not put her children ahead of her job. But some have simply had to admit that *other people are better with them at this stage than I am.* Again, not all moms are June Cleaver. Even women who work part-time have agreed with me that the time spent away from round-the-clock child care gives them a much-needed break and allows them to come back to their children with a refreshed and better attitude. But, alas, I have a feeling that Dr. Laura would consider these attitudes a cop-out. I heard her tell a caller once: "Kids don't much care if you're happy. They only care that you're there." I'm not so sure about that.

Would you like to spend 24 hours a day with someone who was unhappy? Would you like to spend every waking moment with someone who didn't want to be there? I certainly wouldn't, and I don't think that kids would either. Everyone needs a break — even stay-at-home moms who are thrilled to be there. We don't all need or want full-time work schedules, but we all need time to pursue our own interests.

I later made the decision to cut out child care almost entirely and work from home, and I made that decision as much for me as for my daughter. *I wanted* to spend more time with her. She was doing just fine on my part-time work schedule. Whenever I would go pick her up, I would find her laughing and having a good time. She was in excellent care (and I'm not just saying that because my mother-in-law will probably read this!). My point is that our children deserve the best possible care. Sometimes Mom is the best suited to provide that care and sometimes she isn't. I like to think that I'm the best thing for my daughter right now, but the truth is that she gets tired of me, too! We're both learning as we go, just as most families do, and a change of pace benefits everyone.

FORGIVENESS

MANY CALLERS to Dr. Laura's show talk about forgiveness. Many want to know if they are obligated to forgive someone who has wronged them. As I understand Dr. Laura, there are three criteria for forgiveness, which she refers to as the three R's: Responsibility, Remorse and Repair. That is, in order to be forgiven, the wrongdoer must first accept responsibility for his actions, must show genuine regret and then must take some action to repair any damages done. Also, one cannot forgive someone for something that was done to someone else. Only the person who has been wronged can do the forgiving.

Often I have heard Christian callers say things like, "I know I should forgive him, but." Dr. Laura promptly cuts them off and reiterates the requirements for forgiveness. But she is missing something. This is, in my opinion, one of the finer distinctions between Judaism and Christianity. Dr. Laura's view is understandably the traditional Jewish perspective. However, Christianity teaches that the followers of Jesus should learn to forgive as Jesus forgave. They should learn to forgive no matter what. They should treat their enemies as Jesus would have treated them.

Personally, I lean more toward the Christian side on this one. But I think that there is a bit of a problem with semantics here. It's one thing to allow someone back into your life after a betrayal. This, I agree, requires the three R's and might never include *forgetting*. But I consider "forgiveness" to be something much more spiritual in nature.

We have all had experiences with people who have treated us badly. People betray us, people use us and sometimes people are just downright evil to us. But to me, forgiveness means looking beyond the events and actions of the physical realm. It means looking at the situation from the soul's perspective and figuring out what lesson can be extracted from the pain of the physical event. Sometimes the lessons are very difficult to discern. Sometimes it takes years for the lesson to surface. But there is always a lesson. Forgiveness means understanding how even people who hurt us or make us angry are contributing to our growth and development as spiritual beings. We have wonderful opportunities to learn when we examine how we react to our enemies. I believe that this is the forgiveness that Jesus was talking about and that Christians are encouraged to practice.

ADDICTION AND COMPULSION

A MAN CALLED DR. LAURA recently about his wife. They had been married about 16 years, I think. He was concerned because his wife had a habit of hiding bills that came in the mail and he described how he would discover boxes of unopened mail hidden in closets. The problem was obviously hurting the family because he could not trust his wife to be honest about their finances. Dr. Laura suggested psychoanalysis. She described the woman as having an abnormal compulsion. She immediately recognized the condition as a mental problem and urged the man to get his wife some help.

Most psychologists have no problem diagnosing obsessive/compulsive disorders. People who suffer from them display such behaviors as washing their hands until they crack and bleed or checking and rechecking appliance switches. They might have obsessive germ paranoia and be afraid to touch anything. These people are recognized as having a sort of disorder. They are not viewed as character flawed. They are not viewed as weak or self-indulgent. After all, they would stop if only they could, right? And thus they need help, right? Even people who suffer from such afflictions as agoraphobia, who cannot bring themselves to step outside their homes, are not spurned by society or called "bums."

Yet Dr. Laura seems to have an entirely different view of people with some other sorts of compulsions or addictions. For example, people who are addicted to drugs or alcohol are portrayed by her as weak, the implication being that they could stop their habit at any time if only they cared enough about themselves and/or their families. The same could be said for people with compulsive gambling habits or compulsive sexual habits.

Many times I've heard Dr. Laura dismiss the notion of sexual addiction as nonsense. She has claimed that there is no such thing, that it is merely a character issue. I'm not so sure. Because of the stigma attached to such a problem and probably because most people believe as Dr. Laura does, I doubt that most people seek any help for this problem. I think that this is unfortunate. I have known people who have had deviant sexual compulsions, and I can say with confidence that none of them eagerly give in to their "addictions." They are consciously aware that what they have felt and, in some cases, have done is wrong. I have even heard of pedophiles who have begged not to be let out of prison because they know that they are not capable of controlling their compulsion. This does not sound like a character flaw. It sounds more like a request for help.

I believe that the same is true for people with drug or alcohol addictions. Aside from the very real physiological addictions associated with these drugs and alcohol, I believe that these people suffer as much as someone with obsessive-compulsive disorder. Again, I think that you would be hard pressed to find many people with serious drug problems who would say that they enjoy their habit.

Most will tell you that they would like very much to quit.

I'm referring here to people with true and serious addictions or compulsions. I'm not talking about someone who is merely self-indulgent and looking for an excuse to make poor choices. I'm not a psychologist, but I can imagine that it is difficult to make the distinction.

My point is that drug and alcohol addictions are viewed by most people as simply personal problems. It is assumed that if people really wanted to stop, they would stop. People with uncontrollable sexual obsessions are often just labeled "perverts." They are simply snickered at and joked about or just viewed as scum of the earth. Again, it is assumed that if they wanted to, they could stop. I find it interesting that no one says this about the person who washes his hands 50 times in an hour.

I wonder how many people would be able to change their destructive behavior if they were to be treated by a psychologist or psychiatrist in the same manner as someone with an obsessive-compulsive disorder is treated.

MISCELLANEOUS QUOTES

"WE THINK OF OURSELVES as being omnipotent during the week." Dr. Laura used this line as a prelude to a discussion on the need for religion in our lives. Her point was that because we all feel this way, we need religion to bring humility back at the end of the week. I would like to ask her sometime about those of us who do not feel omnipotent — those of us who know that we are only human and not above others.

****

Dr. Laura writes, "Consider the proliferation of fraction-ated groups (feminists, gays and lesbians, foreign ethnic group — American, adult child of some bad experience, disabled by addictions, and such) of people with individual-ized agendas, angers, demands, and expectations based upon the notions of oppressions, hardship, prejudice, and entitlement. These days, folks seem to be ... making unbelievable and excessive demands, focusing inward. ... This mode breeds discontent in those who would be better prepared to take on challenging opportunities with a dose of optimism, instruction, compassion for others, and the understanding that focus and hard work have built many a bridge over a seemingly impassible river."

First of all, I would like to point out that there is a difference between recognizing misdeeds of the past and continuing to live as victims of them. After all, the wrongs that have been done by certain groups to other groups cannot be overcome unless we are willing to examine them and learn from them. We cannot simply sweep aside generations of oppression and pretend that it did not occur. It wasn't very long ago that women were oppressed in this country. While we have made great strides through focus and hard work, there are still some very real obstacles for many women, obstacles that can only be overcome by shining a bright and public light on the problem.

Many people of non-white heritage still suffer as victims of hate and ignorance. But there are people who want to forget all of the past. Many people claim that to remember the true history of the United States is to tarnish its image as a great nation. A man once complained to me that his third grade son was learning in school about all of the horrible things that the Europeans did to the Native Americans in the past. He thought that it was appalling that his son was being taught that his ancestors committed such unspeakable acts. *Well,* I told him, *we really did that! We really did all but wipe them out for the simple reason that we were not willing to co-exist peacefully with people whose spirituality and way of life was different from our own.* How else shall we put it?

It wasn't that bad, he huffed back to me. Wasn't it? I hope that he isn't also one of those people who claim that the holocaust was grossly exaggerated and really not such a bad thing.

One of Dr. Laura's fractionated groups — gays and lesbians — are accused by some of making excessive demands by insisting that they should be allowed to marry whom they choose. I have yet to understand what is so excessive about that demand. Wouldn't *everyone* like to be able to marry whom they choose? The argument, of course, is that such a union should not be recognized as equivalent to that between a man and a woman. "It's not what God intended," some people will say. I've also heard that same argument used against interracial marriages as well — and it's still ridiculous. The distinction we need to make here is between the religious institution of marriage and the legal and social institution of marriage.

I can understand certain churches refusing to marry homosexual couples. Many religions teach that homosexuality is forbidden by God. While I disagree with that position, I can respect a church's decision to not recognize the marriage on religious grounds. What I cannot respect is the refusal to recognize any two people who choose to enter the *legal* institution of marriage. The legal and social benefits of marriage are extended without prejudice to any man and woman. There are tax benefits, group health insurance benefits, pension benefits and power of attorney benefits that are automatically bestowed upon legal spouses. I see no reason why these benefits should not include *any* two spouses. No one is asking that people accept the marriages on religious terms — only on legal terms. Unfortunately, this is an issue that "a dose of optimism" has yet to make an impact on.

The second point I would like to make regarding that quote from Dr. Laura is that she does not recognize herself as one of the whiners! One of the largest growing groups of complainers in this country are the ultraconservatives — for example, those who complain constantly about how the public school system is brainwashing their children or who whine about how movies, television and music are corrupting society. They, along with Dr. Laura, are even getting upset over car commercials and carpet cleaning coupons! Dr. Laura insists on her program that parents be at home to raise their children, and yet, she still seems to think that the parents' influence can be easily undermined by a television show like *Dawson's Creek*. I have confidence that the values that I instill in my children will have the logic and structure to withstand such exposure.

The ultraconservative approach is an attempt to make life conform to something safe and secure, to make it fit neatly into a pretty little package. Anything that threatens the perceived notion of what life should be is branded as evil or corrupt. Any and all means are used to discredit or destroy. Unfortunately Dr. Laura is becoming more and more "agendized" all the time. She seems to have slowly been sucked in. It seems to me that more could be accomplished with a dose of optimism, a little instruction, and, above all, more compassion for others.

****

Dr. Laura writes, "When someone mistakes you for someone else, there is an uncomfortable sense of losing importance, or that all you have done and have become becomes discounted or lost. Moreover, when someone has or uses your same name, you feel threatened or diminished." I was thoroughly confused by this comment. I'm not sure where this perspective comes from, but it can only be rooted in insecurity.

I have been mistaken for someone else a number of times — I just have one of those familiar faces, I guess. When it happens I do not feel like I am less important. In fact, I do not even think about myself at all. I am usually feeling compassion for the person who has made the

References

Quotes from the Dr. Laura radio show are from the author's memory. Every intention is that they are accurate in word as well as in context.

Other quotes were obtained from the following published sources:

The Ten Commandments — The Significance of God's Laws in Everyday Life — By Dr. Laura Schlessinger and Rabbi Stewart Vogel. Copyright 1998 by Dr. Laura C. Schlessinger — Published by HarperCollins

Zen — A Way of Life — By Christmas Humphreys. Copyright 1962 by Christmas Humphreys — Published by NTC Publishing Group

Reference was also made to the following:

The Seat of the Soul — By Gary Zukov.
Conversations with God — By Neal Donald Walsh

I would also like to thank Mike Lombardi for his permission to include his work.